CW00762031

books by
BOXER

www.booksbyboxer.com

Published by
Books By Boxer, Leeds, LS13 4BS UK
Books by Boxer (EU), Dublin D02 P593 IRELAND
© Books By Boxer 2022
All Rights Reserved
MADE IN CHINA
ISBN: 9781909732896

This leaf-saving guide belongs to:

_____

You've picked up this book, that only means one thing - you really suck at keeping houseplants alive. You water, water, and water again, but your whole planting experience turns into a flop consisting of of dying leaves and shrivelled up flower buds.

But don't lose the pot just yet! This fun and informative guide will turn your withered weedlings into prospering plants in no time!

Happy plant parenting!

"*Plants*
GIVE US
Oxygen
FOR THE
Lungs
AND FOR THE
Soul."

— TERRI GUILLEMETS

Air You Ready to Grow?

AIR PURIFYING PLANTS

HELP TO DETOXIFY YOUR AIR AND MAKE YOUR HOME A CLEANER SPACE WITH THESE PURIFYING PLANTS!

Spider Plant

Pothos

Peace Lily

English Ivy

Areca Plant

Keep Your Furry Friends Free From Danger!

PET SAFE PLANTS

EVEN IF YOU CAN'T LOOK AFTER YOUR PLANTS, THE LEAST YOU CAN DO IS LOOK AFTER YOUR FOUR-LEGGED FAMILY WITH THESE PET-SAFE PLANTS!

Rattlesnake

Boston Fern

Orchid

Coconut Palm

Chinese Money Plant

"NO OTHER LIFE
Is as pure as
THE PLANTS.
It is no wonder
WE CANNOT
UNDERSTAND THEM."

- ROBERT BLACK

ZZ Plant

OTHER NAMES: ZANZIBAR GEM, ZUZU PLANT, ETERNITY PLANT

Water Me:

Once every 2-3 weeks, watering more in brighter light, and less in lower light!

How Much Sun:

Bright, indirect sunlight for most of the day! Find a room with south facing windows, and place it out of direct sunlight!

Top Tip:

The ZZ Plant is an extremely easy plant to keep, making it one of the most popular houseplants out there! Just try to protect it from getting too cold... brrr!

DID YOU KNOW:

This plant is sometimes called a 'Fat Boy Plant', because of its thick, fat bulb!

Yucca

OTHER NAMES: SPINELESS YUCCA, SOFT-TIP YUCCA, ITABO

Water Me:
Once every 10-14 days! Make sure the roots aren't sitting in water, and ensure that the top few inches of soil are dry to touch!

How Much Sun:
The more the better! As a desert plant, the yucca thrives in as much sunshine as possible, so in sunnier months, your plant botanical buddy can join you in your garden and sunbathe during the day!

Top Tip:
Mix the soil with sand to better support the yucca plant and help the sturdy cane stay upright!

DID YOU KNOW:
The yucca plant is so iconic to Southern and Central America, that the yucca flower that can be found on wild species is the State Flower of New Mexico!

Venus Fly-Trap

OTHER NAMES: DIONAEA MUSCIPULA, VENUS'S FLYTRAP

Water Me:

This freaky plant needs to be watered every two to four days, depending on the season. The soil needs to be moist at all times, but not waterlogged.

How Much Sun:

A venus fly-trap needs at least four hours of direct sunlight daily, and around 12 hours of bright light a day.

Top Tip:

The fly-trap thrives in 'bad' soil. Soil which is acidic and damp, but also has good drainage is best. They also require no nutrients, so stay away from potting soil, fertiliser and compost!

DID YOU KNOW:

The venus fly-trap is a carnivorous plant, feasting on small bugs, spiders and flies. That being said, feeding this plant the same meat we eat will cause this plant to rot and die (so no burgers!).

I'M NOT SURE HOW MANY
PLANTS IT TAKES
TO BE HAPPY,
BUT SO FAR IT'S
NOT FIFTY SIX.

String of Pearls

OTHER NAMES: SENECIO ROWLEYANUS, STRING OF BEADS

Water Me:

Sensitive to overwatering, this quirky plant should be watered around every two weeks, allowing the soil around its roots to dry out completely.

How Much Sun:

This little plant enjoys both direct and indirect sunlight. Place it in direct sunlight in the mornings, but move to an indirectly sunny spot in the afternoon.

Top Tip:

Ensure to prune this plant every once in a while as its vines can easily become heavy and make the top look sparse.

DID YOU KNOW:

These plants can bloom in the summer months - producing daisy-looking flowers that let off a sweet fragrance similar to cinnamon!

Spider Plant

RIBBON PLANT, ST BERNARD'S LILY, SPIDER IVY

Water Me:

Spider plants like to be watered about once a week, but wait till the top of the soil is dry to the touch first!

How Much Sun:

Bright spaces with indirect light works best – so whack your spider plant by a bright window or patio door!

Top Tip:

Much like you on your last holiday, spider plants can burn easily! Even in indirect sunlight, if you water your spider baby in the middle of the day the fragile leaves can get scorched! Water in the morning or evening to take best care!

DID YOU KNOW:

Native to Southern Africa, the spider plant gets its name because of its smaller, spider-like plant babies that dangle from the mother plant, like little spiders hanging on a web!

Snake Plant

OTHER NAMES: MOTHER IN LAW'S TONGUE

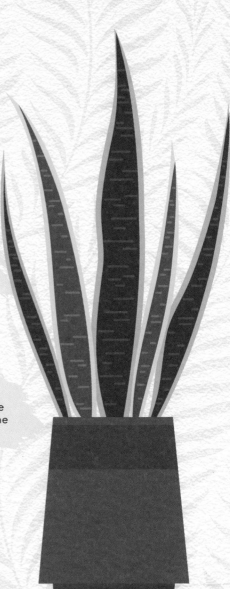

Water Me:

Every 2-3 weeks, allowing for the soil to go bone dry before re-watering!

How Much Sun:

The snake plant is relatively versatile, but is best in bright, indirect sunlight. It can hack a little bit of direct sunlight, but like your own human child, it should be monitored in case it burns!

Top Tip:

Plant these in a soil that drains well – despite being almost indestructible, they can be prone to root rot!

DID YOU KNOW:

Snake plants are actually a large type of succulent, and can last for over a month without water! However, this isn't advised... come on... show it some love!

Rubber plant

OTHER NAMES: FICUS ELASTICA, RUBBER FIG, RUBBER BUSH, RUBBER TREE, INDIAN RUBBER BUSH, INDIAN RUBBER TREE

Water Me:
Every one to two weeks, allowing the soil to dry out in-between watering.

How Much Sun:
The rubber plant thrives in medium to bright indirect sunlight, but can actually tolerate direct sunlight too!

Top Tip:
Remove any dying leaves and branches from your plant to improve its appearance and help keep it healthy!

DID YOU KNOW:
The latex sap from the rubber plant was once used to make rubber balls, clothing and even shoes! Its rubber is now used in many items including surgical gloves, pacifiers and car tyres!!

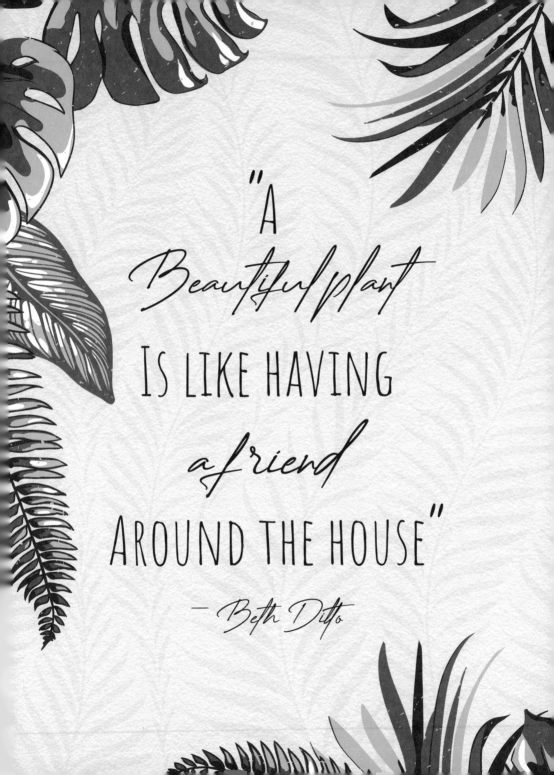

Rattlesnake Plant

OTHER NAMES: GOEPPERTIA INSIGNIS, PRAYER PLANT

Water Me:

The rattlesnake plant needs watering frequently in summer, but needs the top layer of soil to be dry before watering in the winter months.

How Much Sun:

Filtered light is best for this plant, but placing in a bright room away from direct sunlight works just as well!

Top Tip:

The perfect temperature for this plant is around 70 degrees Fahrenheit, and exposure to temperatures below this can make the plant wilt and die.

DID YOU KNOW:

The rattlesnake plant can move its leaves ever so slightly to manage its own light and water intake!

Pothos

OTHER NAMES: GOLDEN POTHOS, MONEY PLANT, DEVIL'S IVY

Water Me:
Every 1-2 weeks, depending on sunlight exposure.

How Much Sun:
20-25°C - 12 hours of indirect light for prime conditions!

DID YOU KNOW:
This plant got the nickname 'Devil's Ivy', because it is nearly impossible to kill, surviving in nearly pitch-black conditions, as well as over and under watering - perfect if you have a dodgy track record!

Philodendron

IT IS POINTLESS LISTING THE PHILODENDRON VARIETIES – THERE ARE OVER 450!

Water Me:

Philodendrons love a generous soak once every week during spring and summer, and once every 10 days to two weeks in winter – if you want to treat it, give the leaves a light mist a few times a week too (because it's worth it!)

How Much Sun:

Medium light, and bright indirect sunlight!

Top Tip:

Older philodendron leaves tend to turn yellow naturally. However, if you begin to notice multiple yellow leaves at one time, this may be in indicator that the plant is getting a little too much sun.

DID YOU KNOW:

Philodendron flowers release pheromones that attract male beetles in the wild, which are responsible for their pollination – saucy!

Peace Lily

OTHER NAMES: WHITE SAILS, SPATHE FLOWER

Water Me:

At least once a week - the great thing about a peace lily is it sags slightly when it needs watering, so just try to be a little observant and listen to your lily!

How Much Sun:

The Peace Lily is the perfect way to brighten up a darker room or corner, as they do best in low to medium, indirect light - so long as there is a big window close-ish!

Top Tip:

If your peace lily gets brown tips, it may be because you are over or under watering! Try to listen to your plant, and when it wilts, don't wait too long before watering it, otherwise its leaves will go brown!

DID YOU KNOW:
As its name suggests, the peace lily is an international symbol of peace and hope, and the white, porcelain flower is the symbol of the white flag!

Orchid

SCIENTIFIC NAME: ORCHIDACEAE

Water Me:

Once a week during winter, twice a week during summer.

How Much Sun:

Orchids thrive in 12-16 hours of bright, indirect sunlight, each day – greedy!

Top Tip:

Notoriously difficult to keep, many people say that you cannot kill an orchid, as the orchid always kills itself – charming! If I were you, I'd stick to the plastic variety.

DID YOU KNOW:
There are more than 25,000 species of orchid in the world!

Monstera

OTHER NAMES: SWISS CHEESE PLANT, HURRICANE PLANT, SPLIT-LEAF PHILODENDRON, MEXICAN BREADFRUIT

Water Me:

Monstera should be watered every one to two weeks, with soil drying in-between watering sessions!

How Much Sun:

Bright, indirect sunlight will let this plant thrive! Keep it near a window but away from the sun's rays to see the full benefits.

Top Tip:

This tropical plant needs humidity to survive. A humidifier will work its magic to control the health of this pretty plant!

DID YOU KNOW:

Monstera leaves have natural slits to allow heavy rainwater to pass through without damaging the plant - perfect for tropical storms!

Maranta Plant

OTHER NAMES: MARANTA LEUCONEURA, PRAYER PLANT, PRAYING HANDS

Water Me:
Every one to two weeks, letting the soil dry around halfway before watering again (they can be sensitive to hard tap-water).

How Much Sun:
Maranta plants thrive in bright, indirect sunlight, but can tolerate a bit of shade if needs must!

Top Tip:
A humidifier will work wonders in keeping your maranta healthy, because they prefer humid conditions!

DID YOU KNOW:
These plants have a quirky ability that allows it to follow the sun throughout the day with their large, vibrant leaves!

Lucky Bamboo

OTHER NAMES: DRACAENA BRAUNII, FRIENDSHIP BAMBOO, CURLY BAMBOO, CHINESE BAMBOO, CHINESE WATER BAMBOO

Water Me:

Water this plant once a week. If only placing into water, ensure it's sitting in a few inches at all times. If planted in soil, give it a happy medium (not too moist or too dry).

How Much Sun:

This bamboo needs indirect sunlight to survive - direct sunlight will scorch its leaves!

Top Tip:

Sometimes tap water can be too hard for this plant. If you notice brown tips or a white build-up in the container, switch to distilled water instead!

DID YOU KNOW:

The lucky bamboo is said to be just that, lucky. In Chinese tradition, the amount of luck is monitored on the amount of stalks you have - 2 for love and doubling luck, 3 for wealth, happiness and a long life. Each quantity has a different meaning!

LET'S

Root

FOR EACH OTHER AND
WATCH EACH OTHER GROW!

Grow!

Lady Palm

OTHER NAMES: RHAPIS EXCELS, BAMBOO PALM, MINIATURE FAN PALM

Water Me:

Once a week, or when the top of the soil feels dry.

How Much Sun:

The unfiltered sun can cause sun damage to this plant, so place in bright light away from the direct sun.

Top Tip:

Repot this bushy palm every two years, to ensure it doesn't outgrow its pot!

DID YOU KNOW:

The lady palm is native to China, but it is not certain if it still exists in the wild.

Jade Plant

OTHER NAMES: CRASSULA OVATA, FRIENDSHIP PLANT, MONEY PLANT, SILVER DOLLAR PLANT

Water Me:

This plant should be watered every two to three weeks, as jade plants are succulents and store water in their leaves!

How Much Sun:

Jade plants need at least six hours of bright light a day. Older (and larger) jade plants can handle direct sunlight, but younger plants should only have indirect sunlight.

Top Tip:

Try not to splash your jade plant's leaves when watering, as this can make your plant susceptible to fungi.

DID YOU KNOW:

The jade plant is seen as a good luck charm throughout Asia, and is thought to bring wealth and prosperity - pop it close to your home's entrance to test its luck!

Heart Leaf Philodendron

OTHER NAMES: SWEETHEART PLANT, PARLOR IVY, PHILODENDRON SCANDENS

Water Me:

This plant's soil should be kept moist during the summer, and dried out before watering in winter.

How Much Sun:

This romantically named plant is pretty durable and can handle low light, but bright, indirect sunlight is more ideal!

Top Tip:

These plants are known to be sensitive to changes in temperature, and even cold water can shock the plant. Let tap water stand for 24 hours before watering to avoid a drastic temperature change and help remove unwanted chemicals.

DID YOU KNOW:

This beautiful plant contains calcium oxalates – which in turn can cause irritation to your skin and can cause stomach issues if ingested!

Fiddle Leaf Fig

OTHER NAMES: FICUS LYRATA, FICUS PANDURATE, FIDDLE-LEAF FIG, BANJO FIG

Water Me:

Soil needs to be kept evenly moist at all times, though it must not be overwatered. Water a little, two to three times a week!

How Much Sun:

Fiddle leaf figs require bright light, but direct sunlight can burn them. Dull areas will stunt their growth too, so balance is key.

Top Tip:

This lovely plant is toxic to cats and dogs, so keep it away from your fluffy friends!

DID YOU KNOW:
A fiddle leaf fig houseplant can grow up to 2 feet a year - reaching between 6 and 10 feet overall!

Sorry I can't Come, my plants Need me.

English Ivy

OTHER NAMES: COMMON IVY, HEDERA HELIX

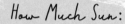

Water Me:

Wait for the soil to dry - this means it should usually need a water 2 times a week.

How Much Sun:

English ivy loves bright, indirect light during warmer months. In cooler months, move it closer to the window for a greater level of light exposure!

Top Tip:

Use a mister to water your ivy - it does better being under than over watered! Just spray a light mist over the plant until the top 2 inches of soil are damp!

DID YOU KNOW:

Despite having a romantic reputation, the English ivy is actually a bit of a thuggish plant bully, and was even banned for sale in the US state of Oregon in 2010!

Dracaena

OTHER NAMES: THIS PLANT WAS SUPPOSEDLY NAMED AFTER THE GREEK WORD FOR FEMALE DRAGON, AND SO HAS MANY VARIATIONS OF ITS NAME SUCH AS DRAGON PLANT AND DRAGON TREE!

Water Me:

Every one to two weeks is suitable for this plant to be watered, as long as the soil stays damp but not wet.

How Much Sun:

This smart plant can grow in low and medium lighting, but thrives the most in bright indirect sunlight!

Top Tip:

Dracaena can be sensitive to fluoride and salt, so it's often better to water with distilled water.

DID YOU KNOW:
There are over 40 variations of this plant, and studies by NASA have shown dracaena can help to remove certain harmful gases from the air.

Coconut Palm

OTHER NAMES: COCOS NUCIFERA

Water Me:

The coconut palm needs frequent watering at around one to two times a week - its soil needs to be moist but not dripping wet!

How Much Sun:

Unlike other plants, the coconut palm actually thrives in direct sunlight, so any kept inside need to live near windows (and moved around if necessary!)

Top Tip:

If you really want your coconut palm to thrive, take it outside for the summer! - They tend to live longer and grow bigger with exposure to the outdoors!

DID YOU KNOW:

Coconut palms are quite resilient to pests when living in their native islands in the Western Pacific, but indoors they are much more susceptible.

Chinese Money Plant

OTHER NAMES: PILEA PEPEROMIOIDES, UFO PLANT

Water Me:
Once a week, but wait for the soil to feel mostly dry between watering!

How Much Sun:
The Chinese money plant loves bright, warm spaces, so pop it by a window for best results!

Top Tip:
Yellow leaves can be the sign of over-watering – but are also a natural sign that the leaves are shedding – don't worry if this is the case! New green leaves will grow back to replace the old yellow ones!

DID YOU KNOW:
This plant is sometimes called the pancake plant, because of the shape of the leaves! Don't try eating the leaves though... they probably won't taste much like pancakes!

Chinese Evergreen

OTHER NAMES: AGLAONEMA

Water Me:

Every 7-10 days - make sure the soil is dry around 2 inches down!

How Much Sun:

Too much direct sunlight actually turns the leaves of this plant yellow! This plant thrives in slightly cooler, darker areas with indirect light, making it a great low maintenance option for lazy plant-lovers and shut-ins!

DID YOU KNOW:

There are over 50 types of aglaonema, with different coloured leaves, but all relatively easy to keep! The Chinese evergreen has distinctive white striped green leaves, and is one of the best varieties for air-purifying!

"I BE-LEAF
IN YOU."

- ANONYMOUS

Cast Iron Plant

OTHER NAMES: ASPIDISTRA ELATIOR, BAR-ROOM PLANT

Water Me:

Once a week at most - you should wait
until the soil has almost dried
out before re-watering.

How Much Sun:

This plant cannot tolerate direct sun, but is as
tough as its name states and can grow even in
a dull room away from windows!

Top Tip:

This plant is one tough cookie and can take
negligence with a pinch of salt. As long as you
don't overwater or place in direct sunlight for an
extended time, this plant will survive!

DID YOU KNOW:
The cast iron plant can live up
to 50 years!

Calathea Ornata

OTHER NAMES: CALATHEA PINSTRIPE, PINSTRIPE PLANT

Water Me:

Every 1 to 2 weeks. This plant hates being in completely dry soil, so try to check the moisture in the soil on the regular!

How Much Sun:

Liking slightly more dim and humid environments, pop your calathea Ornata in well-lit areas, but out of direct sunlight!

Top Tip:

Famously finicky, the best tip to give is to not get too emotionally attached to it! Even houseplant pros have a love/hate relationship with this demanding plant, and if you take the plunge, prepare yourself!

DID YOU KNOW:

This plant is sometimes called the 'Prayer Plant', because in the darker hours, the leaves can fold upwards, giving the appearance of praying hands!

Bromeliad

OTHER NAMES: BROMELIACEAE GENERA (EACH SPECIES HAS A DIFFERENT NAME)

Water Me:

Once a week is fine for most variations of bromeliad, and although they prefer moist conditions, allowing the soil to dry a little in between watering can help if the plant looks over-watered.

How Much Sun:

Every variation is different. Those with soft, flexible leaves enjoy dull areas more, whilst those with stiff, hard leaves prefer bright indirect light!

Top Tip:

These funky, exotic plants can be quite top-heavy, so ensure it's placed in a heavy pot to avoid it toppling over!

DID YOU KNOW:

There are over 2,700 variations of bromeliad, the pineapple being one of them!

Boston fern

OTHER NAMES: NEPHROLEPIS EXALTATA, SWORD FERN

Water Me:
Once a week, keeping the soil damp but not soaking wet!

How Much Sun:
Boston ferns thrive most in medium and bright indirect sunlight (They're highly adaptable!)

Top Tip:
Adding additional humidity to this plant, especially in the winter months, can do wonders for its prosperity - due to its tropical origins!

DID YOU KNOW:
The Boston fern consists of around 30 different varieties, and is a native to tropical environments!

I'm Sexy
AND I
Grow it!

Bamboo Palm

OTHER NAMES: CHAMAEDOREA SEIFRIZII, REED PALM, CLUSTERED PARLOR PALM, CANE PALM

Water Me:

These palms should be kept evenly moist, but can be sensitive to both over and under watering. Let the top of its soil dry out between watering.

How Much Sun:

These tropical palms don't require bright light to thrive, so are suitable for medium to low light conditions!

Top Tip:

These plants are susceptible to common pests, so make sure to check its leaves and stem often!

DID YOU KNOW:

This plant is more than just a pretty 'vase', NASA actually has them listed on their clean air varieties list!

Asparagus Fern

OTHER NAMES: SPRENGER, FOXTAIL, DWARF, COMPACT SPRENGER

How Much Sun:

Almost all the different kinds of asparagus fern require similar care – great for us lazy plant lovers! Much like an OAP on a summer's day, the asparagus fern grows best in some sunshine during the morning, but some cooler shade in the afternoon!

Water Me:

Once or twice a week – wait for the soil to be semi-dry, but not bone dry as this may stunt your fern's growth!

Top Tip:

Water more sparingly in autumn and winter, and feed once a month with liquid plant feed in spring and summer to watch your fern prosper!

DID YOU KNOW:

Unlike a regular fern, the asparagus fern produces star-shaped flowers that turn into lovely berries – great for adding a pop of colour into your home!

Areca Palm

OTHER NAMES: GOLDEN CANE PALM, BUTTERFLY PALM, YELLOW PALM

Water Me:
Every one to two weeks when placed in a bright space, but older plants need watering less regularly.

How Much Sun:
Areca palms do well in tropical areas, so at least six hours of indirect daylight per day is ideal!

Top Tip:
By placing an areca palm in your bedroom, it will purify the air as you get your beauty sleep!

DID YOU KNOW:
Though areca palms can be found in the Western Caribbean and Florida, they are native to Madagascar!

Anthurium

OTHER NAMES: FLAMINGO FLOWER, HAWAIIAN HEART, PAINTED TONGUE, PAINTERS PALETTE

Water Me:

Only water your anthurium every once a week or so, as these tropical plants actually dislike too much water and can rot easily if kept in waterlogged conditions.

How Much Sun:

These gorgeous plants enjoy lots of light, but not direct sunlight.

Top Tip:

Keep this plant in warm temperatures – anything under 60 degrees Fahrenheit can kill this beautiful plant.

DID YOU KNOW:
The colourful flowers on these plants aren't actually flowers, but a shield-like leaf called a 'spathe' that protects the plant.

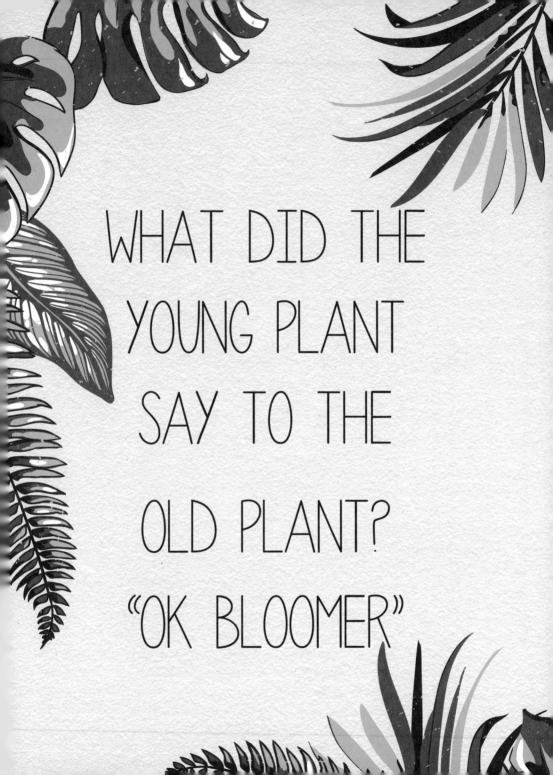

WHAT DID THE YOUNG PLANT SAY TO THE OLD PLANT? "OK BLOOMER"

Alocasia

ALOCASIA MYCORRHIZAS, ELEPHANT EARS, AFRICAN MASK

Water Me:

These plants enjoy consistent moisture, but like to partially dry out between watering too (soggy soil can make the plant susceptible to fungal infections).

How Much Sun:

How much sun this plant likes wholly depends on the variation. Some plants are more sun-trained than others, but most appreciate indirect sunlight.

Top Tip:

This plant requires a humid environment to survive, so keeping it away from drafts, air conditioning and cold spots can work wonders to help this plant thrive!

DID YOU KNOW:

The leaves on the alocasia are highly toxic to both humans and animals, and can cause death if consumed - be warned.

Air Plant

OTHER NAMES: EPIPHYTE, LIFE PLANT, TROPICAL PLANT

Water Me:

2-3 times a week. Use a mister and spray a few times a week. Air plants should also take a longer 1 hour soak every week for best care! However, be sure to keep an eye out for overwatering – make sure your plant is completely dry before giving it a drink!

How Much Sun:

Bright but indirect light. Don't pop these on a sunny windowsill - they may get fried!

Top Tip:

After giving your air plants a nice soak, try to let them air dry in a slightly brighter spot than their usual home for an hour or so, otherwise they might start to rot!

DID YOU KNOW:

Air plants get their name because they don't require soil, and in the wild (In South and Central America) can be found growing on trees, cacti and rocks!

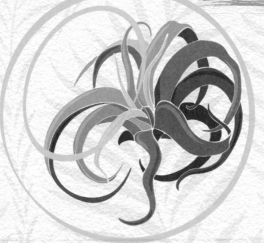

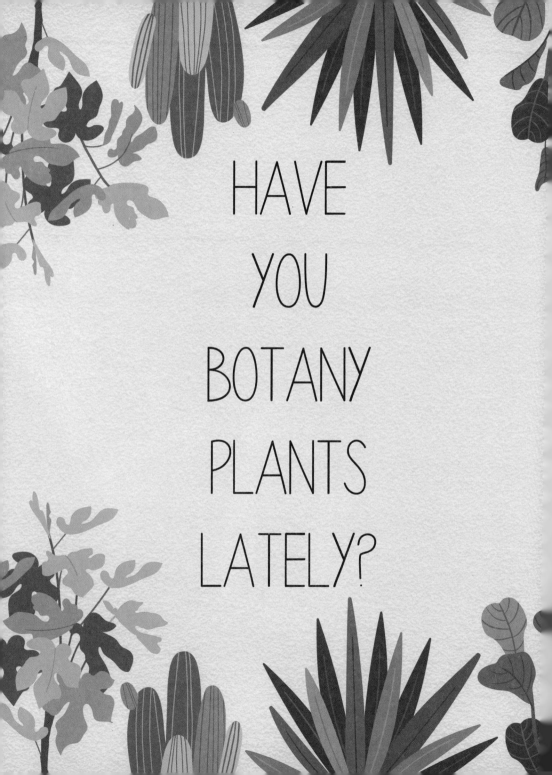

Houseplant Heaven

SO YOU'VE TRIED YOUR VERY BEST TO KEEP YOUR PLANT FROM MEETING IT'S UNTIMELY FATE, BUT NOTHING HAS WORKED AND YOUR ONCE VOLUMINOUS PLANT IS NOW JUST A DRY TWIG IN THE SOIL. PERHAPS IT'S TIME TO JUST GIVE UP AND CALL IT A LESSON LEARNED FOR NEXT TIME. WHY NOT DISPOSE OF YOUR NOW DEAD PLANT IN ONE OF THESE USEFUL WAYS?

Pop your plant into a compost heap so it can live its life through other plants.

Use the decaying leaves to create a piece of art – like a paint covered sponge.

Sprinkle old leaves into your other less-dead plants soil to keep them thriving.

Use the empty plant pot as an excuse to go buy another plant.

Humidity Heals

MOST PLANTS LIKE A GOOD HUMID CLIMATE, SO IF YOUR PLANTS ARE LOOKING A LITTLE DOWN IN THE DUMPS, IT MIGHT BE GOOD TO CONSIDER ONE OF THESE CLIMATE TACTICS…

Move rooms

If your plant is currently residing in the living room or hallway, it could be a good idea to move it into the kitchen or bathroom for the time-being. These two rooms often get steamy, and might give your plants some oomph!

Cover it up

Make your own DIY rose from Beauty and the Beast by covering your plants with a see through glass or container. Most plants release carbon monoxide, which if isolated can make an area more humid!

Green house

If you're out of ideas and none of the above are working, you could invest in a small greenhouse and hope for the best.

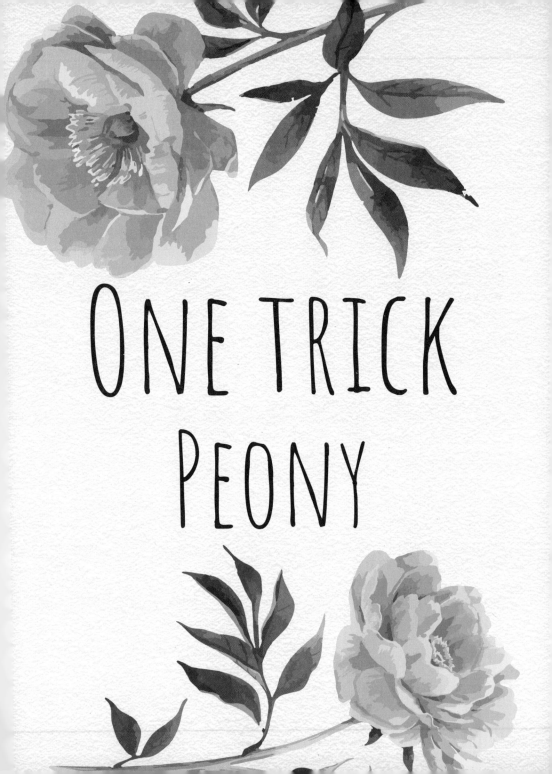

ONE TRICK PEONY

Soggy Solutions

IF YOUR PLANT HAS BEEN WATERED, WATERED, AND WATERED AGAIN,
CHANCES ARE IT'S FEELING A BIT SOGGY FOR ITSELF! ALL IS NOT LOST
THOUGH, IF YOUR PLANT STILL HAS SIGNS OF LIFE, IT MIGHT BE WORTH
TRYING ONE OF THE FOLLOWING SOLUTIONS...

Purge your plant

Your plant is a bit wet but has no signs of stress.
Pour out any excess water, and purge your plant till
the soil dries out a little.

Repot

So your plant is looking a little water dama
now... there's still hope (somewhere). Buy a
pot and soil, and let your plant start fresh.
don't overwater it this time!

Time For a Trim

If your plants are looking a little brown and dull, it could be time for a 'haircut'. Remove any old, dead stems, leaves, and dying flowers to keep the rest of your plant healthy and prospering.

Try to trim your stems back to the healthy part - if possible. Dying or dead leaves and flowers should pull off easy enough, but there could be small sections left behind.

These should be trimmed back to make way for new leaves to grow and flowers to bloom.

Prepare for Winter

IT'S IMPORTANT TO PREPARE YOUR PLANTS FOR THE WINTER MONTHS, SO THEY CAN EASE INTO THE COLDER WEATHER GRADUALLY AND STAY HEALTHY FOR THE SUMMER!

Here's how:

Reduce the water intake for dormant plants.

Move the plant so it gets more sunlight in the darker months.

Give their leaves a clean - so they can take in the light.

Keep them warm by insulating pots with a fabric wrap.

Move them away from drafts and cold spots.

Check for any pests who want to hide from the cold.

Fungus Gnats

FUNGUS GNATS ARE TINY BLACK FLIES THAT FLY AROUND YOUR PRECIOUS PLANTS AND CAUSE HAVOC, WITH THEIR LARVAE FEEDING ON ANY DYING PARTS OF YOUR PLANTS.

Fungus Gnats are attracted to:

- Waterlogged plants
- Mould
- Damp, warm environments
- Bright lighting

They can be controlled using hydrogen peroxide and water – which is completely safe for your plant!

Ensure the top of your plant's soil is dry.

Take 1 part peroxide, 4 parts water and mix.

Pour the mixture into the plant pot until it comes out of the base.

Keep your plant isolated from others for 2-3, weeks or until you're sure all gnats have gone.

Repeat when necessary.

Naturally Fertilised

BRING YOUR PLANT BACK TO LIFE WITH NATURAL FERTILISERS! YES, OLD FOOD SCRAPS AND EVEN HAIR CAN HELP YOUR PLANTS THRIVE AT ITS VERY BEST (EVEN IF IT LOOKS HALF DEAD RIGHT NOW)...

Just some natural fertilisers:

- Eggshells
- Coffee grounds
- Green tea grounds
- Banana peels
- Freshwater aquarium water (if you have one)
- Hair

Basically, anything that can be put into a compost heap can be used to make your plants prosper - maybe stay away from the manure though...

Soil Saboteur

SOMETIMES THE ISSUES YOUR PLANTS ARE FACING ISN'T NECESSARILY DOWN TO YOUR PLANTS, BUT THE SOIL IT SITS IN. IF YOUR SOIL IS STRUGGLING TO HOLD WATER, CHANCES ARE, YOUR PLANT WILL BE IMPACTED.

Soil is old

If the soil has been used and reused for some time, it might have had its day! So, out with the old and in with the new... before your plant suffers!

Soil is too compact

If your soil is packed solid in your pot, wat won't be able to get to the lower layers. Tr removing some soil and fluffing the rest o gently with a small garden fork (whilst no harming the plant's roots)

Soil has too much peat mo

Peat moss is a great addition to soil, once it dries out, it struggles to get again - making your soil unabsorbe

Soil is too dehydrated

Add some compost to your potted soil to bring some life back into it. This should help your soil reabsorb some water

Sticky Leaves

DOES YOUR PLANT HAVE STICKY, GUMMY LEAVES?

DON'T THROW IT OUT JUST YET, THIS COULD BE DOWN TO PESTY INSECTS!
OBTRUSIVE INSECTS SUCH AS APHIDS, MEALYBUGS AND OTHER HOUSEPLANT
PESTS CAN SUCK THE SAP OUT OF PLANTS.

BY USING SOAP (NOT WASHING-UP LIQUID) AND WATER, YOU CAN WASH THE PLANT
TO TRY AND REMOVE ALL THE INSECTS.

BUT BE CAREFUL, IF JUST ONE SINGLE INSECT SURVIVES,
YOUR PLANT WILL SOON HAVE ANOTHER INFESTATION,
AND THEY CAN MOVE ONTO OTHER PLANTS IN YOUR HOME!

Wilting Leaves

IF YOUR PLANTS LEAVES ARE LOOKING A LITTLE WORN AND WILTED, DON'T PANIC JUST YET, THIS COULD BE THE REASON WHY:

Overwatering

Is the soil wet? Drain any excess water and water less frequently.

Under-watering

Is the soil dry? Give it a drink and ensure to water when necessary!

Too much sun

If your plant is sunbathing, take it out of direct sunlight.

Too much heat

Place your plant in a cooler room out of direct sunlight.

Air too dry

A humidifier will help replace moisture in the air, especially in summer!

Plant Parenthood

Crispy Leaves

DOES THE SOUND OF YOUR PLANT'S LEAVES RESEMBLE THE CRUNCHING OF CRISPS IN A CINEMA? SEEMS LIKE YOU HAVE A SERIOUS CASE OF CRUNCHY LEAF. NOT TO WORRY, THERE'S HOPE FOR YOUR PLANT YET!

Here could be some reasons:

Overwatering
Is the soil soggy? Remove excess water and water your plant less.

Under-watering
Does the soil feel dry? Water it and keep up when necessary!

Too much fertilisation
Too much fertiliser can harm your roots, which effects the whole plant's health.

Problem with the soil
It could be that you're using the wrong kind of soil (or the soil is too loose). Check and change your soil if needed!

Too little space
If your pot is too small, it can stop your roots from taking up enough water. Get a bigger pot!

Dead Leaves at Base

DOES THE TOP OF YOUR PLANT LOOK AS HEALTHY AS CAN BE, BUT THE BASE LOOKS LIKE IT'S READY TO RETIRE? DYING LEAVES AT THE BOTTOM OF YOUR BELOVED PLANT MIGHT CAUSE YOU TO WORRY, BUT IT COULD BE SOMETHING SIMPLE...

Ageing

As they age, plants will shed their bottom leaves to allow for new leaves to take their place. So if it's a slow change, don't worry just yet.

Light changes

If the plant has recently moved to another spot in your home, this can cause your plant to rapidly lose its bottom leaves. Move it back!

Lack of water

If your soil is damp, check your roots for anything that could be stopping them from taking in water like root rot or soil being too compact.

Black and Squishy Leaves

DOES YOUR PLANT LOOK A LITTLE… WELL, UM… MANKY? LEAVES TURNING BLACK AND SQUISHY (AND POSSIBLY A BIT SMELLY TOO)? THIS COULD BE WHY:

Overwatering

Drain the pot of water and water less regularly.

Too much fertiliser

Change your soil and use less fertiliser (each plant needs a different amount).

Fungal Damage

Remove any damaged leaves and treat with a fungicide.

Soil is too acidic

Check the PH scale of the soil and apply phosphate fertiliser if needed.

Frost damage

Remove the black leaves and move the plant away from cool spots like cold windows.

Sunburn

Move your plant to shade and give it a little more water.

Pest infestation

Wash the plant with soap and water, and use insecticides if necessary.

Pale Leaves

IF YOUR PLANT'S LEAVES ARE LOOKING A LITTLE PALE AND PEAKY, YOU FIRST NEED TO CHECK IF IT'S JUST A NEW LEAF GROWING OR IF IT'S SOMETHING MORE SINISTER. IF IT'S THE LATTER, DON'T WORRY TOO MUCH, YOUR PLANT CAN BE BROUGHT BACK TO HEALTH!

Under-watering

If your soil is dry, your plant could be thirsty.
Water it more often!

Too much sun

If your plant is left in direct sunlight, there is a chance that it is burning. Move it off that windowsill!

Not enough sun

If your plant is in a shady corner of your home, it might be longing for a brighter place.

Pest infestation

Give your plant a bath in soap and water - only use insecticides if necessary!

IT'S PARTY

THYME!

Do Dry This at Home!

YOU'VE GROWN YOUR VERY OWN HERBS - CONGRATULATIONS! WHY NOT PUT THEM TO GOOD USE AND TRY YOUR HAND AT DRYING THEM? IT'S NOT AS SCARY AS IT SEEMS, JUST FOLLOW THE BELOW STEPS AND YOU'LL BE ON YOUR WAY TO SEASONING EVERYTHING YOU EAT!

Low-moisture herbs such as sage, thyme, bay leaves and rosemary (to name a few) are best air-dried. Simply trim your fresh herbs at an angle to avoid damaging the rest of your plant.

Now you can prepare to bundle your herb's branches together. Remember, the less branches you have in a bundle, the quicker they'll dry. 5-10 branches is a good quantity to begin with.

Find a perfect spot to hang your bundles. This is ideally a dark, cool and dry place like a pantry or under-stairs cupboard.

Hang your bundles stem side up to allow your herbs to dry quicker and fully. You should allow around seven to ten days to dry.

Once your herbs leaves sound crunchy when crushed, you're good to go! Seal your herbs in separate airtight containers to keep them fresh!

Herb you had greenfingers!

THERE'S NO HASSLE WHEN IT COMES TO POTTING HERBS, CONTRARY TO POPULAR BELIEF. WITH THESE SMALL STEPS, YOU CAN BE ON YOUR WAY TO A PARSLEY PARADISE!

Pick a pot.

Fill the pot with moist soil ¾ of the way up and poke holes into the soil for your seeds.

Plant your herb seeds - six inches apart or 2-3 seeds in each pot.

Pat down the soil gently to ensure your seeds can grow happily.

Cover your pots with plastic wrap - to stop your seeds from drying too much.

Water (the soil should be moist but not soggy).

Top tips:

Herbs need plenty of light - so approximately 6 hours of direct sun a day can do your herbs wonders!

You can grow your herbs in just about anything which has a drainage hole - toilet rolls, plant pots or even last night's takeaway tray!

Thyme to Grow

THE BEST THING ABOUT GROWING HERBS INDOORS IS THAT MOST HERBS CAN BE PLANTED ALL YEAR ROUND! HOWEVER, CERTAIN HERBS ARE SUITED TO SURVIVAL IN DIFFERENT CLIMATES:

Hardier herbs, such as rosemary, lavender, thyme and oregano can hold their own in cooler temperatures, and so may work well in winter!

Oregano

Lavender

More leafy herbs, such as basil, tarragon, chives and coriander do well in direct sunlight, and will thrive when planted in summer!

Tarragon

Coriander

What's the Big Dill?

NOT ONLY ARE HERBS GREAT FOR COOKING WITH, THEY MAKE YOUR HOUSE SMELL GREAT, AND ARE SURPRISINGLY EASY TO KEEP (EVEN YOU MIGHT BE ABLE TO BE A HERB-PARENT!)

Best herbs for your house:

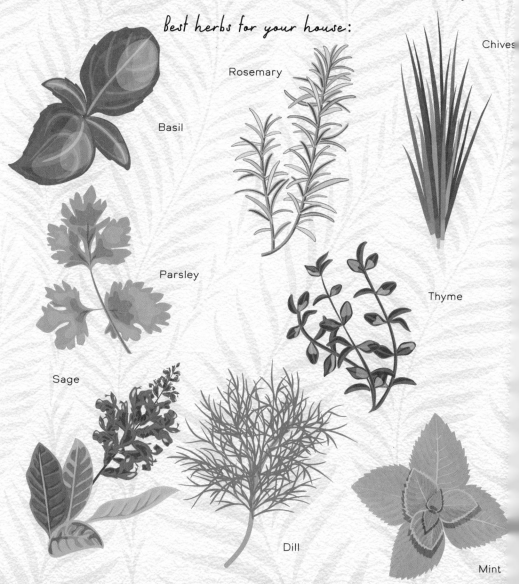

Basil

Rosemary

Chives

Parsley

Thyme

Sage

Dill

Mint

DON'T KALE MY VIBES

GOOD CHIVES ONLY

Vase Your Responsibilities

WHEN LOOKING AFTER FLOWERS, A LOT OF PEOPLE FALL AT THE FIRST HURDLE! DID YOU KNOW THAT A DIRTY VASE CAN HARBOUR LOADS OF GROSS BACTERIA THAT CAN CUT YOUR FLOWERS' LIVES SHORT?

To clean your vase:

Fill your vase ¾ of the way up with warm water.
Next, add in a tablespoon of baking powder,
Then add a good dash of white vinegar – you should start to see some fizzing and bubbling, which is exactly what helps to remove the residue from inside your vase!

Then rinse, and pop your flowers in as usual!

Don't be lazy - try to change the water every so often, and clean your vase between changes, to give your flowers the best shot at a long and prosperous life!

Aspirin-kle of Love!

A POPULAR RUMOUR AMONGST BUDDING GARDENERS (SO, MAYBE YOU, MAYBE NOT) IS THAT AN ASPIRIN IS GOOD FOR YOUR PLANTS, ESPECIALLY CUT FLOWERS!

Well, the rumours are true! Crushing an Aspirin into the water of your vase will help the water stay cleaner and free of bacteria for longer! This is because of the salicylic acid in the tablet.

Hopefully horticulture can be headache-free!

FLOWERS ARE
FOR TINDER DATES,
PLANTS ARE FOR
SOUL MATES.

Snip Only the Tip

SOMEONE BOUGHT YOU FLOWERS? AWW. HOW SWEET. NOW THE NEXT STEP IS TO MAKE SURE THEY LAST LONGER THAN ONE NIGHT!

To best prepare your cut flowers, use some sharp scissors, and cut them to size (to fit in your CLEAN vase). Try to ensure there are no jagged edges - these can lead to rot!

en, once they are arranged how you like them, ll the vase with around 5 inches of water, and ve the flowers in a cool, dry place to drink for a v hours, before popping them pride of place in a warmer setting!

Try to store them away in a cool, or cold, setting when you don't want them on show - this will help them last much longer!

Glorious Gladiolus

GLADIOLUS ARE PERFECT FLOWERS FOR WHEN YOU WANT
TO BRIGHTEN UP A ROOM, BUT THEY'LL SOON BE GONE
IF YOU DON'T CARE FOR THEM PROPERLY... KEEP THEM
LOOKING COLOURFUL AND VIBRANT WITH THESE TIPS!

A warm room will allow your Gladioli to open up. But once open, these should be swiftly moved to a cooler spot to keep them fresher for longer.

Remove any leaves that will become submerged with water, to prevent them making the water murky and bacteria-filled.

If some flowers start looking a little dull, it's time to remove thos party-poopers so your other flowers can prosper!

Timeless Tulips

HAS SOMEONE WHO LOVES YOU (OR DESPISES YOU AND WANTS TO SEE YOU KILL YOUR FLOWERS) BOUGHT YOU SOME COLOURFUL TULIPS? SHOW THEM HOW CAPABLE YOU ARE AT LOOKING AFTER A LIVING THING WITH THESE QUICK HACKS!

Tulips are susceptible to getting bubbles in their stems that can cause premature drooping, so prick the stem just under the flower head to ensure a good flow of water!

So there's been a lot of talk about cutting stems diagonally, but be warned, this isn't the case for tulips. Tulips actually like their stems to be cut straight!

If you're running a little low on flower food, a little sprinkle of sugar should be enough to keep them perky and pretty too!

Ice can stop your tulips from blooming too quickly – so you can watch their beauty for longer.

Bewitching Bird of Paradise

THESE EXOTIC FLOWERS LOOK LIKE THEY COULD BE HARD TO HANDLE, BUT WITH THE RIGHT CARE, THE BIRD OF PARADISE CAN LIGHT UP YOUR HOME WITHOUT MUCH EFFORT!

Snip the stem underwater, in a diagonal motion to ensure it can take in enough water for the flowers.

Keep removing any dead leaves and flower heads to help the rest of your flowers survive for as long as possible!

Remove any leaves that might sit below the water's surface to stop the water from going cloudy, bacteria forming, and your flowers prematurely dying off.

You can poppy-n anytime!

Charismatic Chrysanthemums

CHRYSANTHEMUMS ARE FOUND IN NEARLY EVERY BOUQUET OF FLOWERS, AND THAT'S BECAUSE THEY'RE BRIGHT AND VIBRANT. THEY'RE QUITE TOUGH FOR A FLOWER, BUT IN ORDER TO KEEP THEM THIS WAY, YOU SHOULD FOLLOW THESE STEPS:

Snip the stems diagonally so they can drink more water – the shorter the stem, the more water these flowers will take in.

Ensure the base water is at room temperature before adding your flowers, and add a few drops of bleach to the mix to keep bacteria at bay.

Remove all the leaves as these can turn yellow very quickly and make your bunch look half-dead – even when your flowers are still healthy!

Cavalier Carnations

LOOKING LIKE A SHOWER LOOFA, THESE PUFFY FLOWERS REALLY KNOW HOW TO BLOOM! BUT HOW DO YOU KEEP THEM LOOKING MORE BEAUTIFUL AND LESS LIKE AN OLD, SOGGY CABBAGE LEAF?

A bouquet of carnations is a simple yet beautiful gift to receive. That being said, we need to keep them looking that way for as long as possible!

When preparing these flowers, you should chop the stem diagonally and remove any leaves that will sit below water level – to avoid premature death.

Carnations are quite tough, so should do fine without much interference. Make sure they're kept away from drafts and direct sunlight, and chop the stem some more if they're looking a little dull.

Dainty Daffodils

SPRING HAS ARRIVED - WHICH MEANS WE HAVE THESE BRIGHT, UPRIGHT FLOWERS! DAINTY DAFFODILS ARE GREAT... THAT IS TILL YOU TAKE THEM HOME AND THEY FLOP QUICKER THAN YOUR PROMOTION. DON'T WORRY THOUGH - WE'LL HAVE YOUR DAFFS SPRINGING BACK TO LIFE IN NO TIME!

As soon as daffodils are initially cut, they should be placed in warm water and have a few hours to rest before being arranged in a vase. Cut the stems while they are underwater to avoid any air bubbles from forming in the stems.

When placing them into a vase, they sho be kept separate from any other flowe variety, as the sap from daffodil stems i toxic to other flowers. Replace the vase water every two days to preserve them.

Two tablespoons of lemon juice, one tablespoon of sugar and half a teaspoon of bleach in the daffodil's water will help keep them bright and upright for longer!

Daffodils can be toxic to both humans and pets, so be careful handling them and keep out of reach of pets and children.

Astonishing Alstroemeria

THESE EXOTIC FLOWERS LOOK LIKE THEY'VE COME STRAIGHT FROM A 70'S DISCO – THAT BEING SAID, YOU WANT YOUR ALSTROMERIA TO BE 'AH, HA, HA, HA, STAYIN' ALIVE' – OR WHATEVER BEE GEE'S SANG...

Alstroemeria are beautiful flowers, but should be handled with caution to keep them looking lively. When you first receive them, you should wait till the water in your vase is at room temperature, as both cold and warm water can shock them.

Make sure these flowers are kept away from too much heat, cold drafts and direct sunlight, as they can easily be disturbed by changes in temperature – a table in the corner of a room is the perfect placement for these flowers.

Trim the stems at an angle while they are underwater, so the stems don't gain too many air bubbles and so water can easily go up the stems to the flowers – trim the stems every few days!

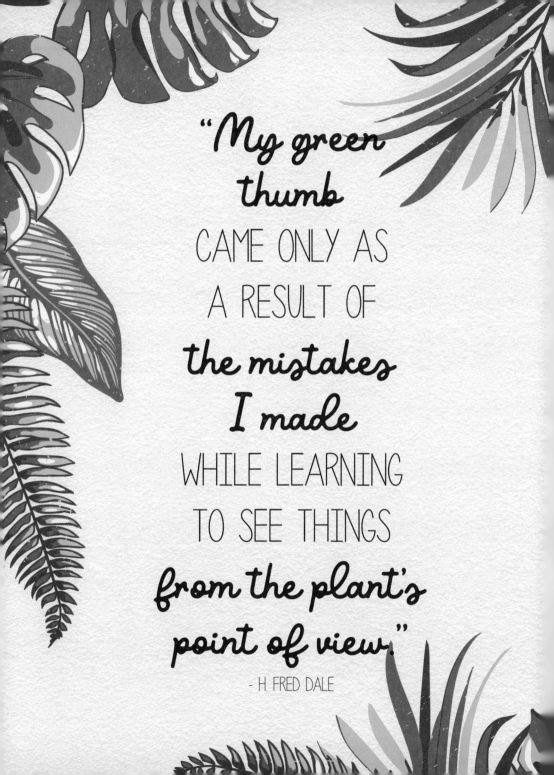

"My green thumb CAME ONLY AS A RESULT OF the mistakes I made WHILE LEARNING TO SEE THINGS from the plant's point of view."

- H. FRED DALE

Sensational Sunflowers

SUNFLOWERS LIKE TO DRINK A LOT OF WATER TO STAY ALIVE, SO KEEPING THEM WELL HYDRATED – EVEN WHEN CUT – WILL ALLOW YOUR SUNNIES TO REMAIN... WELL, SUNNY!

Removing leaves that sit below the waterline is a tip that can help not just sunflowers, but most other flowers, as this can make your flowers rot quicker.

One teaspoon of sugar, two tablespoons of lemon juice, and one tablespoon of vinegar added to your sunflower's water can keep your petals looking vibrant, and can postpone decay in these happy flowers.

Put a small slit in the section of the sunflower's stem that sits underwater, to remove any air bubbles in the stem that could stop an intake of water.

If your sunnies begin to droop, cut their stems short and pop them in warm water to extend their life a little longer!

Luxurious Lilies

WANT TO STOP LILIES LOOKING A LITTLE LIMP? THOUGH THEY'RE THE MOST POPULAR FLOWER BY CHOICE FOR FUNERALS, YOU DON'T HAVE TO LET YOUR CHOPPED FLOWERS KICK THE BUCKET JUST YET!

Lilies really don't want to sit in the same stagnant water till they reach their demise, so don't make the same mistake of most lily recipients – replace the water often to keep your lilies happy.

Lilies are wimps, especially once cut, and the don't respond well to prolonged heat or sunlig – to get the most out of your lilies, store then in a cool, dark place. If there is enough room your fridge, keep them there overnight!!

Pollen can cause issues. With lilies having lots of pollen, any pollen fall can actually eat away at your petals - limiting their lifespan. Try to gently pluck away any pesky pollen - without it touching the petals, of course!

Ravishing Roses

HAS YOUR SIGNIFICANT OTHER GIFTED YOU WITH SOME SAD-LOOKING ROSES, AND YOU WANT TO KNOW HOW TO NURSE THEM BACK TO LIFE? ALL LOVE IS NOT LOST! HERE ARE SOME TIPS AND TRICKS FOR KEEPING YOUR ROSES... ROSY!

Place the roses out of direct sunlight to keep them from drying out! If roses become too dry, the petals will become weak and begin to fall or become limp!

Roses really like warm water, so make sure you change the water regularly with a warm refill!

Roses are very delicate flowers, and so need to be placed in a clean vase! The bacteria of dirty vases can have your flowers looking limp after just a few days!

Harmonious Hydrangea

A FIRM FAVOURITE, THESE BEAUTIFUL FLORAL BALLS CAN BE NOTORIOUSLY HARD TO MAINTAIN, AND HAVE HIGH STANDARDS, MAKING THEM A BIT OF A PRINCESS!

A healthy hydrangea will show a little bit of green under their barky stems, but if your stems are looking a little... well, dead... this may be because you are wrongly watering!

Did you know hydrangeas drink through their leaves, not their stems? To keep these beauties alive, submerge them bloom-first in water for between 20 and 40 minutes! Be warned – if you leave them for over an hour, you may do more harm than good!

Soon your hydrangea will be hydrang-yaas!

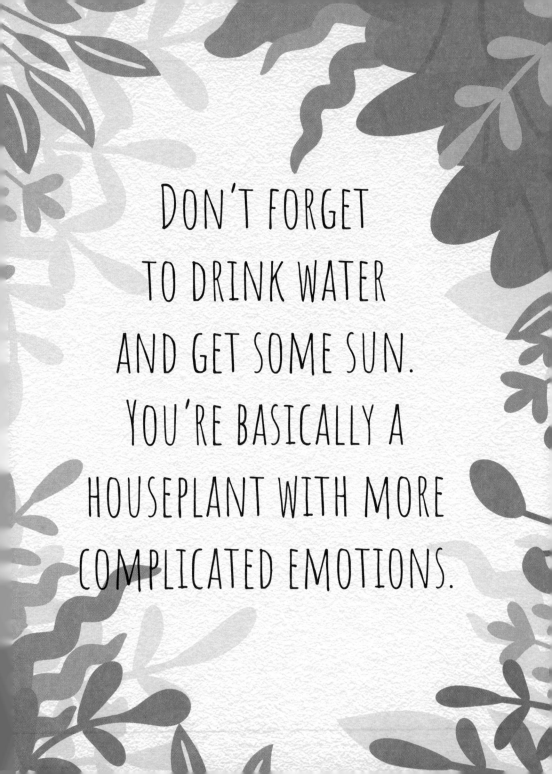

Don't forget
to drink water
and get some sun.
You're basically a
houseplant with more
complicated emotions.

Pack Up Your Fengs and Go A-shui

IT IS NOT JUST ABOUT WHICH PLANTS YOU PUT IN YOUR HOME, BUT ALSO WHERE YOU PUT THEM TO HELP YOU BRING A GOOD VIBE INTO YOUR HOUSE! YOU CAN'T JUST WHACK A PLANT UNDER THE STAIRS AND EXPECT IT TO IMPROVE YOUR LIFE AUTOMATICALLY - YOU NEED TO PLACE YOUR PLANTS WITH PRECISION FOR THE BEST FENG SHUI!

CALLED BAGUA AREAS, THE ENERGY IN DIFFERENT SPACES OF YOUR HOUSE CAN CHANGE THE EFFECTS OF YOUR BELOVED BOTANICALS!

PLACING YOUR PLANTS IN EAST, SOUTHEAST AND SOUTH BAGUA AREAS ARE GREAT FOR OPTIMUM FENG SHUI, DUE TO MAXIMUM SUNLIGHT AND ENERGY EXPOSURE!

THIS IS BECAUSE THE NORTHEAST AND SOUTHWEST AREAS BELONG TO THE EARTH ELEMENT, AND PLACING PLANTS IN THESE SPACES, AS WELL AS THE CENTRE OF THE HOME, CAN WEAKEN THE POSITIVE ENERGIES AROUND THE HOUSE!

Shui That Way

FENG SHUI IS A COMMON PRACTICE THAT INTENDS TO HARMONISE PEOPLE WITH THEIR ENVIRONMENT. SO, EVEN IF YOUR LIFE SEEMS CHAOTIC, YOUR HOME CAN BE A HAVEN FOR RELAXATION AND GOOD VIBES! HAVING HOUSEPLANTS IS A GREAT WAY TO HELP IMPROVE THE FENG SHUI IN YOUR HOME, AND EVERY PLANT HAS ITS OWN USE, BUT BE CAREFUL, SOME POPULAR PLANTS BRING BAD JUJU!

To attract:

Protection:
Mother In Law's Tongue

Wealth and Prosperity:
The Money Tree

Love and Happiness:
Lucky Bamboo
(two stalks for love,
Three for happiness!)

Relaxation:
Philodendron

Air purifying:
Areca Palm

Vera Good Advice

EVEN THOUGH THIS PLANT REPRESENTS HEALTH, THESE PLANTS STILL NEED CARE AND ATTENTION TO STAY ALIVE. IF YOU NOTICE ANY OF THESE SIGNS, YOU SHOULD ACT QUICKLY TO SAVE VERA'S LIFE!

Not draining it - a drainage hole is necessary if you don't want your aloe vera to die a soggy, floppy death.

Not watering enough - aloes don't need loads of water, but they still need some...

Sunny side up - don't put your aloe in direct sunlight or in a dark, shady cupboard. Simple really.

Temperature changes - vera is very sensitive to temperature changes, so keep it in a place where draft or fluctuation is at a minimum.

Soil issues - the wrong kind of soil can upset this plant - make sure you use a fast-draining soil to protect from waterlogging!

Pests - like all plants, insects can be the downfall for this succulent, so inspect it regularly, and take action you notice any creepy crawlies!

Aloe Isn't Vera Well...

YOU GO TO WATER YOUR HANDY ALOE VERA PLANT AND NOTICE IT'S LOOKING A BIT PEAKY. YOU WOULDN'T THINK IT'D BE POSSIBLE FOR THIS MIRACLE PLANT TO SUFFER AILMENTS (AFTER ALL, ISN'T IT SUPPOSED TO CURE MOST THINGS?), BUT POOR LITTLE VERA MIGHT BE ON ITS WAY OUT...

Some possible signs that your plant is poorly:

It seems to be turning brown, yellow or even translucent

Its arms have gone mushy and soft

It's wobbly in the soil

Its arms are drooping

It has brown or red spots on the arms

ALL MIGHT NOT BE LOST JUST YET, BY DETERMINING THE CAUSE AND FIXING THE ISSUE SWIFTLY, YOUR LITTLE ALOE MIGHT STILL HAVE A CHANCE... BUT IF IT'S GONE TO HOUSEPLANT HEAVEN, POP IT IN A COMPOST BIN TO HELP OUT OTHER PLANTS!

Are You Peeling Well?

YOU WANT TO USE ALOE VERA, YOUR NATURAL MIRACLE WORKER, BUT DON'T KNOW WHERE TO START. IT'S NOT ROCKET SCIENCE, AND YOU DON'T NEED MANY TOOLS FOR THE JOB EITHER!

Cut off an arm

Using a sharp blade, slice through the bottom of an aloe arm - careful not to prick yourself.

Once chopped, you'll see a yellow sap ooze out - remove this by letting it drain for 1 hour.

Now wash your aloe arm under cool, running water.

You can now begin to extract the gel

Chop off the sharp edges of the aloe arm first.

Gently remove the skin from the aloe arm by peeling or slicing it off.

Take your leaf and scoop off any aloe gel that remains.

Trim any yellowish layers that remain until a clear pulp is revealed.

One quick rinse, and you're ready to use your aloe vera gel!

No Longer Aloe-ne

YOU HAVE ONE ALOE VERA, BUT WANT TO MAKE IT TWO. WHAT DO YOU DO? IT'S ACTUALLY VERA EASY ONCE YOU KNOW HOW! (EXCUSE THE PUN...)

Pick your poison

Aloe vera can potentially be propagated using a leaf, but this isn't very reliable. We suggest using any offsets the plant already has!

Fly the nest

Once your offset is big enough, you can separate it from the parent plant by first removing dirt from around the offset.

Cut and snip

Use a sharp knife to slice the aloe offset from the parent plant, ensuring some root comes with it!

Plant the pup

Pop this offset into another pot using a fast-draining soil, and wait one week without watering.

Water it

after one week has passed, you can wate your plant and look after it how you woul any other aloe vera!

Pot It Over Vera

ALOE VERA IS A SPECIAL SUCCULENT, SO SHOULD HAVE ITS VERY OWN POT - ONLY THE BEST FOR OUR VERA!

Terracotta or ceramic pots?

A terracotta or ceramic pot is handy for succulents that don't require a lot of water. Due to their breathable properties, you can ensure your lifesaving aloe doesn't get waterlogged!

Tips:

The perfect pot size should be 2 inches larger than the succulent's current size.

Ensure your pot has a drainage hole to allow excess water to drain - aloe isn't keen on taking a bath...

Gritty soil works best for aloe vera plants because it drains well.

If you have a saucer underneath the pot, ensure it is emptied frequently to stop your succ from sitting in a puddle!

Vera Many Uses

ALOE VERA IS THE DOCTOR AMONGST THE PLANT COMMUNITY. A MEDICINAL PLANT, THIS SUCCULENT HAS BEEN USED FOR THOUSANDS OF YEARS TO TREAT MANY AILMENTS, FROM BURNS TO CONSTIPATION! BUT WHAT IS THIS MAGNIFICENT PLANT USED FOR TODAY? HERE'S JUST SOME OF ITS MODERN USES:

Healing burns and scalds - sunburns, spilled tea... you name it!

Oral health - keep your breath nice, teeth clean, and smells at bay with this antiseptic succ!

Immunity increaser – aloe vera is a great help in keeping your immune system at its peak!

Nappy rash - yep. If you have a sore bottom, aloe vera is here to kiss it better...

Muscle pain - aloe vera is a natural anti-inflammatory, so rub it into your aches and pains!

Weight loss - who knew a succulent could help on your weight loss journey!

Acne - found in many facewashes and masks, aloe is a great acne banisher!

Well That Succs

HAVE YOU NOTICED YOUR SUCCULENT LOOKING A LITTLE DOWN IN THE DUMPS LATELY? HERE ARE A FEW INDICATIONS THAT YOUR CUTE LITTLE HOUSEPLANT IS ON ITS WAY TO HOUSEPLANT HEAVEN:

It's all shrivelled up

Its leaves are turning black or red

It has brown spots or brown, mushy leaves

It has droopy leaves

It looks very 'lanky'

It looks dead

SO YOUR SUCCULENT HAS SAID ITS GOODBYES AND NOW YOU'RE LEFT WITH A DEAD PLANT. POP IT INTO A COMPOST HEAP, AND IT MIGHT BRING LIFE TO ANOTHER PLANT ONE DAY!

Don't Succ Too Badly

BEFORE YOU JUMP INTO YOUR ALOE ADVENTURE, YOU SHOULD KNOW THAT IT'S NOT ALWAYS POSSIBLE TO PROTECT YOUR PLANTS. THINGS CAN GO WRONG, THOUGH MOST CAN BE PREDICTED AND SOLVED, AS LONG AS YOU DON'T SUCC TOO BAD...

Not draining your succs - a plant pot without drainage is like you sitting in a bath all day. We go wrinkly, your succulents get root rot.

Misting for moisture - your succulents need water and misting most succs will do nothing but make you look clueless. Just stop.

Not watering enough - your succs are very self-sufficient, but they still need water! Don't dehydrate the poor thing, give it a drink!

Let it shine - as long as you don't put it in the glaring sun, your succ will love you for placing it in a well-lit space.

owded pot - your succulents
n't want to look like sardines
tin - space them out, and for
love of all things planty, don't
x them with non-succulents.

It's Not Pot Luck

IS YOUR SUCCULENT LOOKING TOO SMALL FOR ITS POT? YOU'LL NEED TO BUY IT A NEW HOME AND FIND A COSY NEW SPOT!!

Find a classy new pot for your succulent! (This should be a roomy, well-draining pot)

Gently lift the succ out of its pot – you may want to twist as you pull to make it easier.

Seperate your succulent's roots a little by poking the soil – this is to help your plant grow well in its new pot.

Using a fast-draining soil mix (such as cactus mix), fill your new pot halfway.

Pop your little succulent into new home and cover the root entirely with soil.

Press the soil down gentl

Wait one week before rewarding your succulent w a drink!

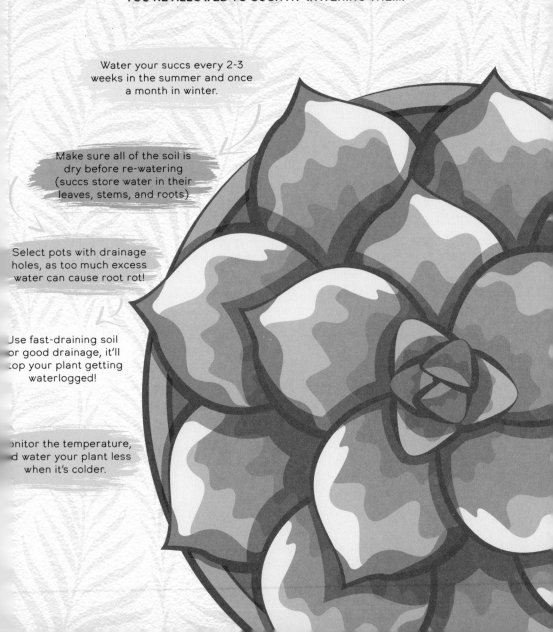

Soaking Succs

SUCCULENTS MIGHT BE MOSTLY SELF-SUFFICIENT, BUT THAT DOESN'T MEAN YOU'RE ALLOWED TO SUCK AT WATERING THEM!

Water your succs every 2-3 weeks in the summer and once a month in winter.

Make sure all of the soil is dry before re-watering (succs store water in their leaves, stems, and roots)

Select pots with drainage holes, as too much excess water can cause root rot!

Use fast-draining soil or good drainage, it'll top your plant getting waterlogged!

onitor the temperature, d water your plant less when it's colder.

Like

PEOPLE,

Plants

RESPOND

TO EXTRA

~~Attention~~

— H. Peter Loewer

Snip and triple!

SO YOU'VE GOT YOUR SUCCULENT AND YOU WANT TO USE SIMPLE MATHS TO TURN ONE SUCC INTO TWO. IT'S NOT ROCKET SCIENCE, JUST FOLLOW THESE EASY STEPS!

Off with your head

Using scissors, snip a 3 inch long section of your plant (one that's covered in leaves)

Plucker up

Individual leaves are another great way to turn one plant into two. Just hold the leaf close to the stem, and ease it off easily by twisting!

Ready to grow

Place your snippets into a dish filled with fast-draining soil, and leave for around 3 days.

Wet and wait

After 3 days, use a spray bottle to squirt everything until the soil is moist (not soaked!). Repeat whenever the soil dries.

Patience... - In about three to four weeks, roots will sprout!

Here we go

Around six to seven weeks after the snip, you'll notice tiny leaves emerging. Your parent snippet might look shrivelled - this is due to it feeding the baby leaves..

Succ These Tips

SO YOU WANT TO TRY YOUR HAND AT KEEPING SUCCULENTS - PERFECT! BUT DO YOU KNOW HOW TO CARE FOR THE LITTLE SUCC-ERS? THESE QUICK TIPS WILL KEEP YOUR PLANT BABIES THRIVING!

Pick a succulent that will stand a chance (starting with a healthy plant makes all the difference!)

Well-draining soil works bes - succulents like to stay dry

Succulents are happy in almost any container that has a drainage hole.

Only water when t soil feels dry – ar drain excess wate

Remove any dying leaves to keep your succulents looking well!

Most succulents love light!

Standard Succulents

Jelly Bean

Though this funky succulent resembles to a packet of jelly beans, it might not taste as good…

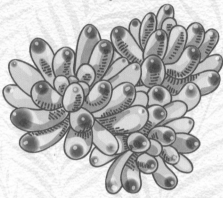

Echeveria

With leaves that have a slight resemblance to spoons, this little plant is ideal for the kitchen sill!

Lavender Scallop

Why's it called a Lavender Scallop? Who knows… but it sure could do with smelling like lavender once in a while!

Debbie

The discoverer of this plant really went all out when naming it. It looks more like a Rose if you ask me.

Standard Succulents

IF YOU'RE CONSIDERING OWNING A SUCCULENT (OR ARE ALREADY BLESSED WITH ONE OF THE LITTLE SUCC-ERS), THEN YOU SHOULD KNOW THE MOST COMMON TYPES!

California Sunset

This flowery succulent looks similar to the Echeveria

Hen & Chicks

With herbal uses, this succ can help treat many things like sunburn and diarrhoea!

Roseum

With rose-tinted leaves, this plant adds a hint of colour to any boring windowsill!

Zebra Plant

Just like the animal it's named after, this plant has bold lines across its leaves!

Tips and Pricks

THOUGH RESILIENT AND FAIRLY SIMPLE TO CARE FOR, THERE ARE SOME THINGS THAT CAN GO WRONG WHEN IT COMES TO LOOKING AFTER YOUR EASY-GOING CACTI...

Treating all cacti the same

Like people, cacti come from all walks of life. One cacti's little is another cacti's lot, so monitor your prickly plant to find out its happy medium.

Too wet or too wilted

Cacti are cool little creatures who store water in their stems! You don't need to water them every day, but remember that they still need an occasional trickle.

Shine a little light

Both too much and too little sunlight can leave your cacti feeling sorry for itself. Open the blinds but keep your cactus at a safe distance from the sun's rays to ensure a happy plant.

Happy home, happy cacti

If your cactus is potted in a cheap, small plant pot with some heavy soil, then chances are, your cactus isn't having a good time. Get it re-potted

Don't bug me

You want to keep your cacti safe from pests, but using harmful pesticides on your precious plants will only cause you trouble. Most cacti actually deter bugs.

You're Potty!

CACTI LIKE HAVING NICE HOMES TOO, YOU KNOW. YOU CAN'T EXPECT IT TO LIVE ITS LIFE IN A SHABBY, SMALL PLASTIC POT AND EXPECT IT TO THRIVE LIKE THE CACTUS IT WANTS TO BE. HELP YOUR BUDDING PLANT LOOK SHARP WITH THESE NEAT PLANT POTS!

Terracotta

TERRACOTTA POTS ARE AMAZING AT KEEPING SOIL DISEASE AND ROOT ROT AT BAY (TWO NASTY THINGS THAT CAN KILL OFF CACTI). ITS POROUS NATURE ALLOWS AIR AND WATER TO FILTER THROUGH TO YOUR SOIL!

Glass terrarium

GLASS TERRARIUMS ARE A FUN WAY TO DISPLAY YOUR PRICKLY PLANTS. HERE'S HOW TO BUILD YOUR OWN:

1. Choose a glass container (one without a lid)

3. Add a layer of mesh (to keep a good structure)

Fill the bottom with a layer of gravel and rocks

5. Pop your cacti into the soil

4. Add cacti-friendly soil on top

6. Use a thin layer of sand on top of the soil and add your favourite rocks!

In a Prickle

SO YOU GO TO WATER YOUR BELOVED SPIKY FRIEND AND NOTICE IT LOOKS A LITTLE WORSE FOR WEAR. IF YOU'RE NOT SURE IF YOUR CACTUS IS STILL BREATHING, THEN HERE ARE SOME TELL-TALE SIGNS YOUR CACTUS HAS KICKED THE POT…

It's all shrivelled up

It has brown, discoloured patches.

It's gone soft and mushy

It's loose and wobbly in its soil (it may even fall over)

It smells dead

IF YOU TRULY THINK YOUR CACTUS IS DEAD, THEN I'M SORRY TO SAY, YOU'RE PROBABLY RIGHT. WHY NOT ADD IT TO A COMPOST HEAP, AND IT CAN HELP ANOTHER PLANT ONE DAY?

Relocation, Relocation

SO YOU WANT TO RELOCATE YOUR CACTUS. WHAT NOW? IT'S NOT AS EASY AS JUST POPPING YOUR SPIKEY FRIEND INTO A NEW POT (THAT WOULD BE TOO EASY), BUT YOU CAN FOLLOW THESE STEPS TO ENSURE YOUR CACTUS STAYS HAPPY AND ON POINT!

Choose a new location.

Pick a pot - cacti like terracotta pots best because they help absorb extra moisture!

Find some ideal well-draining soil - regular soil is no good for cacti as organic materials within it retain water which can lead to root rot.

Add your soil to 1/3 of the pot.

Pop your cactus into its new home.

Fill the remaining space with soil and press the soil down gently.

Give your cactus a drink for a job well done!

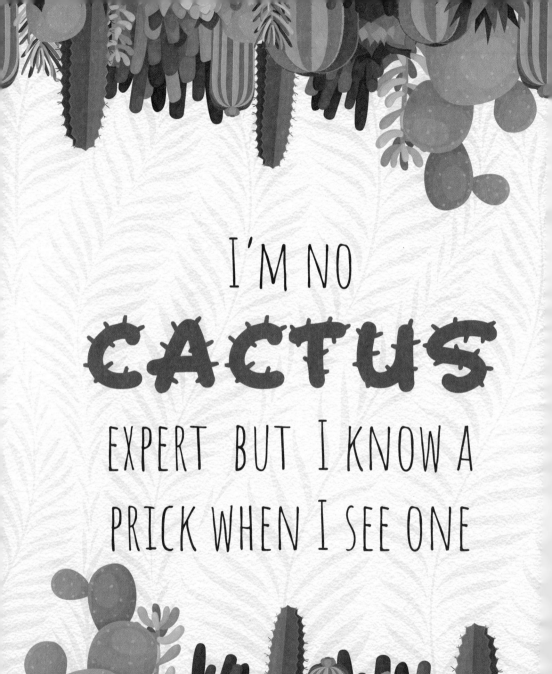

I'M NO

CACTUS

EXPERT BUT I KNOW A
PRICK WHEN I SEE ONE

Desertly Drenched

THINK YOUR CACTI DON'T NEED WATERING?... BAD NEWS MY FRIEND, IT'S A MYTH!

Water your cacti once a week in the summer, but only once a month in the winter.

Your cactus will go 'dormant' in winter, meaning it will pause its growth.

Small, baby cacti need more water (to grow big and strong), but older cacti should be watered less frequently.

Only water your cacti when the soil is completely dry, otherwise you risk overwatering them.

Sun and Spikes

YOUR CACTI LOVES THE WARMTH, BUT THAT DOESN'T MEAN A WINDOWSILL IS THE BEST LOCATION FOR YOUR PRICKLY PLANTS...

Cacti survive and thrive the most when they have a good light source.

Too little sun can make your cactus stressed and it might start looking a little pale.

If your cactus begins to turn brown or yellow in places, it might be getting sunburned from too much exposure to the sun.

Place your cacti in the shade on an evening to protect it from the strong evening sun.

Home your cactus in a brightly lit room, but not in direct sunlight - it'll get a tan!

Common Cacti

Lady Finger Cactus

Looking a little bit cheeky, this long cactus sure knows how to stand to attention.

Bishops Cap

Native to Mexico, this cactus looks like a piece of contemporary art.

Saguaro

This iconic species of cacti can be found in every cartoon featuring a desert...

Blue Columnar Cactus

This funky, blue-hued cactus looks both jazzy and slightly ill too!

Common Cacti

IF YOU'RE JUST STARTING OUT ON YOUR PLANT-OWNING ADVENTURE, THEN A CACTUS IS AN EASY WIN. HERE ARE 8 COMMON CACTI – CAREFUL, THEY'RE STABBY!

Christmas Cactus

This blooming plant doesn't look like your typical cactus, and it's not just for Christmas either!

Barrel Cactus

These spikey balls can be miniature, but have potential to grow up to 3 feet tall!

Moon Cactus

This colourful cactus really does look like something from outer space!

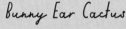

Bunny Ear Cactus

This fun cactus resembles both a bunny and a children's drawing.

"IF A PLANT IS SAD,
DO OTHER PLANTS
PHOTOSYNTHESIZE
WITH IT?"
– ANONYMOUS

Dozy Decor
PLANTS TO HELP YOU SLEEP

DID YOU KNOW THAT SOME PLANTS ARE ACTUALLY GREAT AT HELPING YOU RELAX? POP THESE IN YOUR BEDROOM TO HELP MAKE YOU UNWIND AND DOZE MORE DEEPLY!

Lavender

Peace Lily

English Ivy

Snake Plant

Jasmine

Botanic Bathrooms

BATHROOM FRIENDLY PLANTS

WHILST IT MAY SEEM A LITTLE BIT OF A WEIRD PLACE TO KEEP YOUR PLANTS, THESE ARE GREAT TO ADD A POP OF COLOUR TO YOUR BATHROOM! NOT ONLY DO THEY LOVE MOIST, DAMP AND HUMID AIR, BUT THEY CAN HELP CREATE YOUR OWN LITTLE OASIS - GREAT FOR BRINGING A TROPICAL VIBE INTO YOUR HOME!

Golden Pothos

Alocasia

Air Plant

Heartleaf Philodendron

Aloe Vera

Allergies Succ!

ALLERGY FRIENDLY PLANTS

PLANTS ARE GREAT FOR BRINGING THE OUTSIDE-IN (AND BRINGING VIBES INTO YOUR HOUSE), BUT IF YOU'RE ALLERGY PRONE, SOME INDOOR FOLIAGE COULD BE YOUR WORST NIGHTMARE! THESE PLANT PALS ARE FRIENDLY TO YOUR ALLERGIES - NO NEED TO FEEL LEFT OUT ANY LONGER!

Areca Plant

Peace Lily

The Dracaena

Bamboo Palm

The Lady Palm

Astrological Agriculture
PLANTS FOR YOUR ZODIAC

♎ Libra
String of Pearls

♏ Scorpio
Snake Plant

♐ Sagittarius
Maranta Plant

♑ Capricorn
Jade Plant

♒ Aquarius
ZZ Plant

♓ Pisces
Spider Plant

Astrological Agriculture

FINDING THE PERFECT HOUSEPLANT FOR YOU AND YOUR LIFESTYLE CAN BE TOUGH, ESPECIALLY IF THEY KEEP DYING ON YOU (R.I.P). WHY NOT MATCH UP YOUR COSMOS WITH YOUR CACTUS BY FINDING THE PERFECT PLANT FOR YOUR ZODIAC SIGN... MAYBE THEN YOU CAN STOP KILLING THEM, AND BRING GOOD FORTUNE AND LUCK TO YOU ALONG THE WAY! WHETHER YOU NEED A PLANT THAT MATCHES YOUR DOTING PERSONALITY, OR ONE THAT IS JUST AS INDEPENDENT AS YOU - FIND YOUR MATCH HERE!

♈ Aries
Zebra Succulent Plant

♉ Taurus
Fiddle Leaf Fig

♊ Gemini
English Ivy

♋ Cancer
Peace Lily

♌ Leo
Bromeliad

♍ Virgo
Braided Money Tree

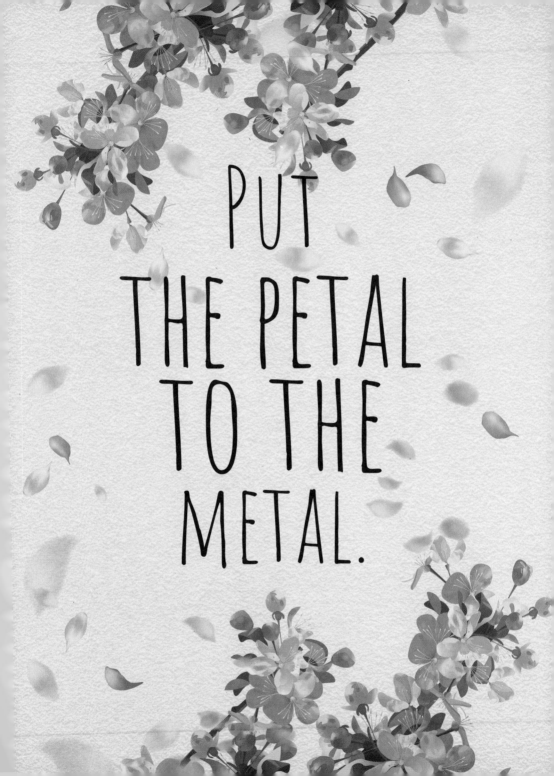

PUT
THE PETAL
TO THE
METAL.

Shut the Blinds!

PLANTS THAT LOVE THE DARK

IF YOU, LIKE MANY PEOPLE, LOVE TO CLOSE YOUR CURTAINS, LIGHT A CANDLE AND BINGE-WATCH YOUR FAVOURITE TV DRAMA... CHOOSE THE RIGHT PLANTS THAT WILL THRIVE IN YOUR HOBBIT HOLE! THESE PLANTS ARE THE PERFECT BOTANICAL BUDDIES THAT THRIVE WITH NO SUNLIGHT!

Chinese Evergreen

Lucky Bamboo

Monstera

Cast Iron

Snake Plant

Sturdy Stems and Resilient Roots

HARD TO KILL PLANTS

IF YOU'VE HAD NO LUCK WITH HOUSEPLANTS SO FAR, MAYBE YOU'RE JUST CHOOSING THE WRONG ONES! THESE PLANTS ARE VERY HARD TO KILL, THANKS TO THEIR ROBUSTNESS AND ADAPTABILITY, PERFECT FOR PEOPLE WHO HAVE A HISTORY OF PLANT-NEGLECT!

Snake Plant

String of Pearls

Jade Plant

Air Plant

Aloe Vera